My Spiritual Awakening: A Journey through the Soul

Lee Knight

BookLeaf
Publishing

India | USA | UK

Presentation by *BookLeaf Publishing*

Web: www.bookleafpub.com

E-mail: info@bookleafpub.com

ISBN: 978-93-5744-957-1

First edition 2022

DEDICATION

To my daughter

ACKNOWLEDGEMENT

I'd like to thank the people who proof-read and encouraged me- poetry and authorship in general is unfamiliar territory. Special thanks to Brogey, Helena, and Ross.

PREFACE

Wonderland and the Underworld are not so very different. Both require soul searching, courage, tenacity, and determination. Both require knowledge and answers that you can only find within yourself. Every person journeys through Wonderland, whether consciously or unconsciously, multiple times in their life. This is the story of one of my journeys.

May you imagine, if you can

May you imagine, if you can
Young and restless, full of empty dreams

Standing on the shores of life
Peering into endless darkness
Imagining the possibilities
Realising too late the danger, falling
Into the emptiness, into the abyss
Total darkness, descending like Persephone, or
Alice
Under the world, through the shadow of the
night
All is silent, except the rushing of the air
Looking for something to hold

All of a sudden, stillness, standing on solid
ground
Walking through darkness until…
Ahead, a light
Knowing there is no other way
Every possibility
Near and yet so far

Imagining knowing all there is to know
Now you know the way forwards
Go, do not look back

Young and restless, full of empty dreams

When I was born
I knew I was safe.
I wanted to learn,
To explore this new place.

When I was one
I wanted to know
What was up high
And how fast I could go.

When I was two
I wanted to speak
My stories, my dreams,
The thoughts I would think.

When I was three
I could pretend
To be a big dog
And dig in the sand!

When I was four
I wanted to grow
As tall as my mum
And watch grown-up shows.

When I was five
I wanted to be
As strong as my favourite
Climbing trees.

When I was six
I started to read
And the world opened up-
Things I couldn't believe.

When I was seven
I hungered for knowledge.
Numbers and science,
And going to college!

When I was eight
I tried the piano.
And cello, and flute,
And even the banjo.

When I was nine
I knew I'd become
A doctor, a singer,
A dancer, a nun!

When I was ten
I wasn't so sure.
The world was so big,
And I was so small.

When I was eleven
My confidence grew.
My body grew bigger,
And my attitude too.

When I was twelve
I couldn't wait
For the world to see
That I'm just so great.

When I was thirteen
I knew for sure
That no one was cooler
Than truly yours.

When I was fourteen,
I knew it all.
I'm smarter than anyone
Ever before.

When I was fifteen
I couldn't imagine
The world without all
Of my future inventions.

When I was sixteen
I wanted independence.
I can work, I can drive,
I don't need my parents!

When I was seventeen
I wanted it all.
I'm so close to freedom,
Do you trust me at all?

When I was 18
I started to see
That I really know nothing.
It's hard being set free.

Standing on the shores of life

Endless, crashing, cold
Waves break on the darkened shore
The cold spray blinds me

Waiting for rescue
I stand on the gritty sand
Only the waves come

The moon shines eerily
Over lonely waves and sand
Nothing can live here

I step in the waves
Suddenly the crashing stops
Everything goes still

Peering into endless darkness

No more waves, I'm standing on air.
Darkness descends and fills my sight-
Endless nothing, darker than night.
Suddenly acutely aware
Of all that's possible and there
Is no way I can ever go
Back to the life I used to know.
And so when all and nothing's true
Nothing remains that I can do
But peer at darkness down below.

Imagining the possibilities

Staring and thinking
Staring and imagining
Imagining doing
Imagining being
Being invincible
Being human
Human and fragile
Human and powerful
Powerful and scared
Powerful and empowered
Empowered to action
Empowered to try
Try to become
Try to be more
More than I was
More than before
Before I was frightened
Before I was unsure
Unsure of my potential
Unsure of my strength
Strength to fight
Strength to prove

Prove my skills
Prove my self
Self love
Self being
Being famous
Being anything
Anything I want
Anything is possible
Possible to fly
Possible to become
Become a teacher
Become a doctor
Doctor of literature
Doctor of medicine
Medicine for the body
Medicine for the soul
Soul mates
Soul journeys
Journeys inward
Journeys downward
Downward spiral
Downward eternal
Eternal life
Eternal possibilities
Possibilities are infinite
Possibilities are mine
Mine...
Infinite…

Realising too late the danger, falling

Oops!
Tripping
Stumbling
Losing my grasp
Darkness swallows me
Nothing to hear or hold
I look down on the abyss
Everything out of my control

Time stretches out before me, endless
Unloved, alone, and defenseless
Filled with fear and emptiness
Everything seems hopeless
Dark night of the soul
Blackness descends
As I fall
Dying
Help

Into the emptiness, into the abyss

Here falls a soul,
Watching itself die.
Not knowing how to save itself,
Unable to fly.
Death has surely come,
The end is surely near.
Accept this fate, this destiny.
There is no point in fear.

Total darkness, descending like Persephone, or Alice

Tumbling, falling, descending, dark.
Like Alice falling asleep in the park.
Like Persephone, walking through the night,
Searching for a beacon shining bright.
The passage of time leaves no mark.

Where does this lead, one might remark.
This journey on which I didn't embark,
My balance I lost, try as I might.
Tumbling, falling, descending.

I strain my eyes to find a spark
Or anything that might landmark
How long has been this endless flight.
I only hope to land upright
And homeward-bound to reembark.
Tumbling, falling, descending.

Under the world, through the shadow of the night

Time freezes
Deep blackness
Gathers round
To witness

Me falling
Down this hole
In myself
Through my soul.

And in me
Darkness sees
What I can't
With great ease.

Inside me
Is a world
With its heart
All unfurled
Under this

Lies the pain
That I must
Feel again.

In my soul
This dark night
Shadows deep
Hide from light

In my mind
In my heart
In my soul
I depart

Time restarts
Suddenly
I realise
Sullenly

Now I'm scared
Now it's real
I don't know
How to feel

I just know
I can't stop
Or slow down
This great drop

Must be brave
Must be strong
Destiny
Can't be wrong

Strong, not weak
Brave, not frail
Fear and shame
Can't prevail

Darkness sees
Silently
Witnessing
Watching me

All is silent, except the rushing of the air

Falling far, falling straight.
Is this a normal character trait
Of falling, that I should fall at this rate?
I start to count- ten, nine, eight…

What is at stake,
And how long will it take
To find a way through this heart ache?

I hope that freedom will be my prize
If from this agony I rise.
It hurts too much to open my eyes.

I never had pain like this before,
I keep counting- six, five, four…
Will I die before I reach one, or…?

Tears threaten from my eyes to spray.
I shut them tight and silently pray
For a hint of light, just a single ray.

Lost in despair,
I have nothing to spare.
Grief and desperation, such a painful pair.
All is silent, except the rushing of the air.

Looking for something to hold

Sometimes it feels
Like you're going to die
Wrong person
Wrong timing
Wrong action
Wrong choice
Desperate loneliness
Seething anger
Raging jealousy
Disconnection
Dissociation
Grief
Your heart being stabbed
Or ripped out
How do you cope
When you can't trust yourself
When you can't trust anyone
When there's nothing to hold
When there's nothing to see
But emptiness
When you're falling
Off a cliff

Or down a hole
With no end in sight
When life seems to pass you by
Because no one cares
No one misses you
No one notices
And no one sees
Your pain

All of a sudden, stillness, standing on solid ground

As if I had never fallen, the ground I keep.
As suddenly as it began, it ends.
The difference I have trouble to tell
Between when I tripped and this new moment.
Darkness wraps around me like a thick coat.

The deafening silence grows impossibly deep,
Unimaginable stillness descends.
I thought the world had stopped when I fell,
Now how I so long for such excitement.
The only sound is my heart in my throat.

Walking through darkness until…

Darkness pulls me, I stumble blind.
I do not know what I might find
Within a darkness of this kind.

The pull so strong, I nearly fall.
I wish that I could loudly call
For help from anyone at all
To tell me where this path may wind.

But I have learnt as I have grown
That no one else has ever known
How strong I can be on my own.
To test my will I am resigned.

So now I let my muscles move
And gradually I find a groove.
Walking confidently I prove
That I can make it through this bind.

I cannot see it with my eyes,
But I trust that a path will rise
And maybe take me by surprise!
But how will the way forwards be signed?

Self-doubt is hard to keep at bay,
So to the universe I pray
For strength as I go on my way.
Onwards, upwards, I now must grind.

I hope the light will make me whole,
And this is now my biggest goal:
Survive this dark night of the soul,
Conquer this dark night of the mind.

Ahead, a light

Behold, a distant light, a beacon in the night,
It shines for all and none to see.
And to my eyes,
Though darkness looms,
Unrelentless, silent, is there nothing that might
Be sweeter or more dear than this-
A shining hope,
The greatest gift.
I can only wonder, was it meant for me?

How can I know beyond all doubt that I should
go,
Follow this mysterious star?
I cannot see
Whence it might come.
As I go on, around each bend, I cannot know
Just how it stays on up ahead.
Is it magic?
And is it real?
How can a light be so near and yet so far?

Never wavering or changing, never different
From what it was when I first saw
The light ahead
My only hope

To find the way, make the shining path apparent.
As the wise men followed their star
So shall I go
Ever asking
The burning question – what is this journey for?

Alas, this shining light that brings me hope is all
That guides me to the final goal.
I do not know
What lies ahead,
I do not know just what dangers I will befall
As I journey towards the light.
I cannot say,
I wish I knew,
What else must I do if I wish to be whole?

Behold! A shining light, a beacon that calls me.
It shines for only me to know
That as I walk
Through darkness deep,
Unending, silent, I will ever clearly see
That nothing is more dear than this-
This shining hope,
This greatest gift.
I know that this is where I am meant to go.

Knowing there is no other way

I must go forwards
And find the light-
There is no other way.

The path winds on,
Around a bend,
There is no other way.

No turning back,
Look straight ahead-
There is no other way.

I must go forwards,
The path winds on,
There is no other way.

Around a bend,
No turning back,
There is no other way.

Look straight ahead
And find the light-
There is no other way.

Every possibility

One is for opportunities hidden by fear.
Two is for passions that you hold dear.
Three is for knowledge you hold in your head.
Four is for skills where your practice has led.
Five is for visions to reach to the sky.
Six is for ambition and strength to try.
Seven is for mindful, consistent work.
Eight is for courage, myself not to shirk.
Nine is for whatever I want to be.
Ten is for everything possible for me.

Near and yet so far

Near yet far, close but distant,
Hopeful but faint.
Closing doors and windows against light
Dreams are close but intangible.
Changing everything, nothing changing.
Tell people stories without wisdom.
Find peace in yourself.
See others ignore truth.
Seek nothing.

Seek truth, ignore others.
See yourself in peace.
Find wisdom without stories people tell.
Changing nothing, everything changing.
Intangible but close are dreams.
Light against windows and doors closing.
Faint but hopeful,
Distant but close, far yet near.

Imagining knowing all there is to know

The darkness is but a test for your mind.
Death watches, silent, you must make a choice.
You feel your eyes open and yet are blind
And you ask yourself, is this my own voice?
But in this still, silent knowledge, rejoice!
Words are important, intention is key.
Darkness is behind, light ahead of me.
Your shadow will tempt you, darkness to wed
But facing the light it's easy to see-
It's all in the blood. Choose right, you ain't dead.

Now you know the way forwards

I fell from the light, from the place I knew
Down a deep, dark hole into the place
Where nothing lives; there was only
A single light to guide me on.
I didn't know how to get back home
And I didn't want to go back to where I came
from.

Now you know the way forwards.

The pain is worse than simply falling
Or losing your balance and scraping your knee.
The soul is wounded and you didn't even know
That that's why you fell- it wasn't your body,
It was your spirit that was injured and needed
To be reborn. Renewed. A fresh start feels like
death;
It can only be found in the darkness,
Contrary to popular opinion and common sense.

Now you know the way forwards.

Your soul will talk if your ego is calm,
Your spirit is wise beyond your mortal years.
Embrace this physical experience
That your soul and your spirit are having
And you will know that everything that happens
Is guiding you onwards towards your soul's
purpose.

Now you know the way forwards.

Go, do not look back

Go, do not look back.
The future winds on, up ahead.
There is nothing that you lack.

Follow the meandering track,
This journey from which your soul has fed.
Go, do not look back.

You will not break, you will not crack.
When all is done and all is said,
There is nothing that you lack.

You need not fear a sneak attack,
Your own worst enemies are inside your head.
Go, do not look back!

The most useful tools aren't in a sack,
Nor something in a book you read.
There is nothing that you lack.

To find the light is not a knack,
It's the purpose of the life you've led.

Go, do not look back!
There is nothing that you lack.

Epilogue

It was once wisely written
That knowledge is a gift.
But I'm not really smitten,
I'm only slightly miffed.

Neither gift nor destination,
Not virtue, or prize on a shelf,
The only knowledge worth contention
Is found within yourself.

A journey in the blackness,
The dark night of the soul.
You won't find better peace than this-
The feeling of being whole.

No one else can do this jigsaw,
No one else can hold the key.
Do not focus on each minor flaw
Or else you will not see.

You will not see your power,
Your strength, your will, your might.
This is your final hour,
This is your chance to fight.

So go! Walk bravely, onward,
Through shadows and through fire.
I'll see you out the other side-
Your own personal empire.